SEP 13 2018

Winchester Public Library
Winchester, MA 01890
781-721-7171
www.winpublib.org

D1305591

EXPLORING
ANCIENT GREECE

by Anita Yasuda

12 STORY LIBRARY

www.12StoryLibrary.com

12-Story Library is an imprint of Bookstaves and Press Room Editions

Produced for 12-Story Library by Red Line Editorial

Photographs ©: D.Bond/Shutterstock Images, cover, 1; Bardocz Peter/Shutterstock Images, 4; Piotr Tomicki/Shutterstock Images, 6; Bradley Weber CC2.0, 7; siete_vidas/Shutterstock Images, 8; Panos Karas/Shutterstock Images, 9; Constantinos Iliopoulos/Shutterstock Images, 10; Tilemahos Efthimiadis CC2.0, 11; turtix/Shutterstock Images, 12; Patrick Gray CC2.0, 13; f8grapher/Shutterstock Images, 14; Breloer Gero/picture-alliance/dpa/AP Images, 15; fab drone/Shutterstock Images, 16, 29; Giannis Papanikos/Shutterstock Images, 17; S-F/Shutterstock Images, 18; Lefteris Papaulakis/Shutterstock Images, 19; Anastasios71/Shutterstock Images, 20, 28; IR Stone/Shutterstock Images, 21; urbazon/Shutterstock Images, 22; Morphart Creation/Shutterstock Images, 23; Everett Historical/Shutterstock Images, 24; Danilo Ascione/Shutterstock Images, 25; RichLegg/Shutterstock Images, 26; Orhan Cam/Shutterstock Images, 27

Content Consultant: Catherine M. Keesling, Associate Professor of Classics, Georgetown University

Library of Congress Cataloging-in-Publication Data
Names: Yasuda, Anita, author.
Title: Exploring ancient Greece / Anita Yasuda.
Description: Mankato, MN : 12 Story Library, 2018. | Series: Exploring
  ancient civilizations | Includes bibliographical references and index. |
  Audience: Grade 4 to 6.
Identifiers: LCCN 2016047641 (print) | LCCN 2016048017 (ebook) | ISBN
  9781632354631 (hardcover : alk. paper) | ISBN 9781632355287 (pbk. : alk.
  paper) | ISBN 9781621435808 (hosted e-book)
Subjects: LCSH: Greece--Civilization--To 146 B.C.--Juvenile literature.
Classification: LCC DF77 .Y37 2018 (print) | LCC DF77 (ebook) | DDC 938--dc23
LC record available at https://lccn.loc.gov/2016047641

Printed in the United States of America
022017

Access free, up-to-date content on this topic plus a full digital version of this book. Scan the QR code on page 31 or use your school's login at 12StoryLibrary.com.

Table of Contents

The Minoans and Mycenaeans Influenced Ancient Greece

The ancient Greeks built the Parthenon, created democracy, and made some of the most important scientific discoveries. How did this impressive civilization begin? People began to settle permanently in southeastern Europe in approximately 7000 BCE. The Grecian peninsula sticks out into the Mediterranean Sea. It is surrounded by many islands, including the Cyclades, the Dodecanese, the Ionian, and Crete.

The ancient Greeks were descended from two groups of people who lived more than 5,000 years ago. They were the Minoans and the Mycenaeans. The Minoans lived

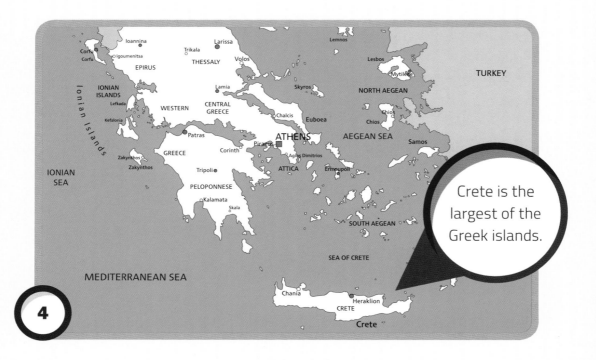

Crete is the largest of the Greek islands.

MINOAN MINOTAUR

Archaeologist Arthur Evans came to Crete in 1900. He uncovered a huge ancient palace at Knossos. To him, the palace looked like a maze. Its paintings of bulls reminded him of a Greek myth. In the story, King Minos was the ruler of Crete. He had a huge maze built for the Minotaur. The Minotaur was a monster with the head of a bull and the body of a man. Evans decided to call the people who built the ancient palace Minoans, after the king.

1,200
Number of rooms the Minoan palace at Knossos may have had.

- The ancient Greeks lived in southeastern Europe.
- The ancient Greeks were descended from the Minoans and the Mycenaeans.
- Trade was important to the Mycenaeans.

on Crete. They were farmers and skilled traders. After a tidal wave hit parts of Crete, their society began to weaken. In time, they were taken over by the Mycenaeans.

The bold Mycenaeans lived on the Greek mainland. The Mycenaean language is believed to be the most ancient form of Greek. Around 1450 BCE, the Mycenaeans became the strongest power in the region. Their cities included Mycenae, Thebes, and Athens.

The Mycenaeans were great sailors. They sailed thousands of miles to trade their goods. They traveled to places as far away as Egypt and Spain. However, around 1200 BCE, their economy began to break down. Invaders may have arrived from the north. Without trade, the Mycenaeans became very poor. Many people fled to the city of Athens. It was one of the few areas that was safe. Others sailed for new homes. They settled around the Mediterranean and founded new colonies. From Athens and from these new colonies, the Greek civilization would soon rise.

The Greeks Created Cities and Colonies

In approximately 800 BCE, a new period in Greek history began. The people living throughout the peninsula started to trade again. Small towns began to grow larger. But only so many people could farm the land. It was rocky, and the soil was poor. So some set out to find new places to start over.

People went east to the Black Sea. Many others left for areas to the west. These explorers lived together in small communities. Greek towns rose up along the coasts of Italy and Sicily. Greek colonies also began in northern Africa, southern France, and Spain. As the Greek world grew, their culture spread. New goods and ideas also flowed back to Greece through trade.

But Greece was not a unified country. Mountains divided areas into small regions. Towns were independent from one another. As they grew larger, city-states began to take shape. Each city-state was called a polis. They had

The mountainous landscape of Greece makes farming difficult.

their own governments and laws. But they also shared many features. The people spoke Greek. They believed in the same gods.

Pottery was decorated with black-figure paintings during the Archaic Period.

Many cities also had a high hill, or acropolis. From that location, people could easily watch for an enemy attack. The ancient Greeks also built their most important buildings there. By the 500s BCE, Sparta and Athens were two of the important city-states. Life in Sparta was based on its army. Life in most city-states focused on agriculture and trade. Sometimes the city-states were allies. They fought together to defeat the Persian army in 480 BCE. At other times, they fought one another for more power.

ARCHAIC AND CLASSICAL

Historians often divide ancient Greece into two time periods. The Archaic Period took place approximately 800–500 BCE. During this time, Greece began to develop a system of government. Cultural similarities between the city-states began to emerge. The Classical Period took place from approximately 500 to 323 BCE. This was the height of ancient Greece.

1,000
Approximate number of city-states in the ancient Greek world.

- The Greeks began colonies in many places.
- Each city-state was independent.
- Sparta and Athens were important city-states.

Sparta Was Powerful

Other Greek city-states feared Sparta. It was known for its strong army. Spartan men spent their lives training to be great soldiers. Men wanted to be brave. They were ready to die for their state.

The process to create such strong soldiers began very early. As soon as children were born, the government inspected them. Weak or ill children were taken away from their parents. These babies were left to die in the wild. But even boys who were

Tourists can see the ruins of ancient Sparta today.

Statue of Leonidas, a Spartan king

family. It was not an easy life. They were given little clothing to wear or food to eat. This encouraged the boys to steal food. Spartans did not think that stealing was bad. During times of war, a soldier might need this skill to stay alive. If a boy was caught stealing, he was beaten. He was punished for not being sneaky enough.

Spartan women also supported the army. The girls of Sparta were encouraged to be strong. They spent time training to be fit and to fight. The Spartans believed that strong women had stronger babies. As the men were away in the army, women ran homes and owned land.

strong enough did not stay with their families for long.

After their seventh birthday, boys left home to learn the skills they would need to fight. They ate, slept, and trained alongside boys of the same age. These boys became their

21
Age men officially joined the army.

- Sparta was known for its strong army.
- Boys left home at seven.
- Girls trained to be fit and strong.

9

4

Democracy Began in Athens

During most of the Archaic Period, Athens was run by kings or the upper class. In 507 BCE, the Athenians created a new form of government they called democracy. People had a say in how things were run. Each free man had a vote. But there was no role for women when it came to government. The Athenians believed that a woman's place was within her own home. Slaves and men who were not born in Athens had no vote either.

Approximately 6,000 free men could participate in the popular assembly.

Ancient Athenians would meet on the Pnyx hill at least once a month.

It was known as the *Ecclesia*. The Ecclesia met on the Pnyx. It was a large outdoor meeting area on a hill. A smaller group of citizens served on the *Boule*. They decided what the Ecclesia would vote on. After listening to a new law, men could speak freely. To vote they raised their hands.

Once a year, citizens met to talk about people who they thought were becoming too powerful. Men came to the assembly with a piece of pottery. It was known as an *ostracon*. They scratched the name of a person who they thought was a threat onto it. The man with the most votes lost. He was sent away from Athens for 10 years.

These ostraca from 486 BCE were votes to exile someone named Megakles.

Citizens also had to serve on juries. Each jury had at least 201 men. They were chosen by lottery. There were no lawyers. So people spoke for themselves. A person with money might hire a speechwriter. After listening to the case, jurors voted. Once the votes were counted, the decision was final.

THINK ABOUT IT

Who makes the decisions in your local government? Investigate online or at your local city hall. Use information on these two pages to decide how Athenian democracy was different from or similar to your local government.

500
Number of men on the Boule.

- Athens had a type of democracy.
- Each male citizen could vote.
- Citizens served on juries.

Myths Explained the World

Why does it rain? Who made people and the earth? Why do the seasons change? The ancient Greeks were curious about the world. They used stories to explain what was happening around them. Greek myths were about a family of gods who behaved like humans but had much more power. Different city-states favored certain gods more than others.

The 12 most important gods were called the Olympians. They lived on the highest mountain in Greece, Mount Olympus. Zeus was the father of many

The Greeks built temples to honor many gods, including this temple for Zeus.

- Myths helped explain the world.
- There were 12 main Greek gods.
- Homer was a famous Greek author.

gods and could control lightning. His daughter, Athena, was the goddess of wisdom and warfare. She was especially important to the city-states of Athens and Sparta. The Parthenon in Athens was built in her honor. Aphrodite was the goddess of love. Poseidon was Zeus's brother and god of the sea.

Many of the myths were about the gods' interest in the day-to-day lives of the people. A god might bring a person success. But an angry god might punish a person. In one story, a girl called Arachne insulted Athena. She claimed that her spinning was better than what the gods could do. Athena wanted to punish Arachne for her arrogance. She turned the girl into a spider. Arachne was doomed to spin her web forever.

Myths were first told out loud. Homer is one of the most famous Greek storytellers. The ancient Greeks believed that he created the poems *The Iliad* and *The Odyssey*. It is more likely that they are the work of more than one person. The poems describe great heroes and battles.

Many artists have illustrated the story of Athena (right) and Arachne.

City-States Held Regular Festivals

The Greeks held festivals to honor the gods. They were lively, fun events with food, sports, plays, and poetry. Festivals were a time for all citizens to take a break from work. Everyone, rich or poor, went to festivals. One huge festival was held in the city of Athens. It was called the Panathenaia. It was a time for everybody to honor Athena. Men, women, and children would march slowly to her temple. They carried with them gifts, such as cakes. Each year, a new peplos, or robe, was made for a statue of the goddess.

In 776 BCE, the first Olympic Games took place. Athletes from every city-state met at Olympia. The site was chosen to honor

Olympia is in ruins today.

Zeus. At the first Olympics, there was only one event. It was the foot race, which was approximately 630 feet (192 m) long. Over time, more events were added to the Games, such as boxing, the long jump, and discus. Athletes could show off their strength and speed. The winners received crowns made of olive leaves. Back at home, they were treated as celebrities.

Olive crowns were used again during the 2004 Summer Olympics in Athens.

Women could not take part in the events. But they could own or train horses for the Games. In 396 BCE, Kyniska became the first woman to receive an olive crown. She owned the horse that won the chariot race that year.

THINK ABOUT IT

What is the largest festival near you? How does it compare to a festival in ancient Greece? Make a list of the similarities and a list of the differences.

60
Number of annual festivals in Athens.

- The Greeks held many festivals.
- Athens held a yearly festival for Athena.
- Athletes from all over Greece competed at the Olympic Games.

Athenian Architecture Reigned Supreme

In 461 BCE, Pericles became a political leader of Athens. He wanted to turn Athens into a great city. He made plans for the construction of several buildings. The Athenians approved of his ideas. Pericles took more than two years to finalize his plans. All this work would take place on a flat-topped hill that rose high above the city. The site is known today as the Acropolis.

The focus of this project was a temple to Athena. She was a symbol of the entire state. Because of its size, workers of all kinds were needed to help. There were teams of carpenters and painters. Thousands of people were hired to build roads and to cut stones. Work lasted for 15 years and was finally finished in 432 BCE. When it was done, the temple, called the Parthenon, could be seen from all over Athens. The

The Parthenon on the Acropolis stands 230 feet (70 m) high.

This entire row of marble sculptures, along with many others, was taken by Lord Elgin.

building's white marble blocks made it gleam.

The temple housed a huge statue of Athena. It was made of gold and ivory. That sent a message to other city-states that Athens was wealthy. Athena was dressed in armor and carried a spear. The statue was removed from the temple sometime before the 500s CE. No one knows what happened to the statue, but some copies survived.

447 BCE
Year work began on the Parthenon.

- Pericles wanted to make Athens great.
- Many buildings were constructed on top of a hill, known as the Acropolis.
- The Parthenon was built to worship Athena.

ELGIN MARBLES

Greek artists created marble sculptures to decorate the Parthenon when it was first created. In the early 1800s, Lord Elgin took about half the sculptures and brought them back to England. Later he sold them to the British Museum, where they are still on display. They are known as the Elgin Marbles. Greece has repeatedly asked to have the sculptures returned to the Parthenon. So far, the British government has refused.

Theater Was Popular

Theater began as a religious festival honoring the god of wine, Dionysus. This festival was held in the city of Athens. Each spring, people were eager to see the plays. Often, there were as many as five plays in one day.

Even prisoners were let out of jail for the festival.

More than 1,500 performers took part. Groups of men and boys sang and chanted stories. Over time, an actor stood apart from the chorus. Thespis is often credited as the

Epidaurus might have had the largest theater in mainland Greece.

first actor. This is why actors are known as thespians today. Later on, plays included three actors and the chorus.

Greek drama was divided into tragedy and comedy. Tragedies were serious plays with sad endings. They dealt with big ideas, such as love and death. Afterward, people watched a short play called a satyr. This type of play made fun of tragic characters. Its actors wore funny costumes, such as horsetails. In comedy, plays made fun of people in power and everyday life.

The Greeks put on plays outdoors. One famous theater was at Epidaurus. The theater was built on the side of a hill. People were seated according to their status. Seats near the front were for important people, such as priests. But there was not one bad seat in the house. Even the back row could hear the smallest murmur on stage.

Ancient Greek comedy mask

14,000
Number of seats at Epidaurus.

- Theater began as a festival for Dionysus.
- Most plays were either tragedies or comedies.
- Epidaurus was a famous theater.

19

Greek Philosophers Figured Things Out

Athens was a center for learning. How should people live? What is the meaning of life? Often people gathered in Athens's marketplace to talk about new ideas. One of these people was Socrates. Socrates never wrote any books. What we know about him today was written by his students.

Socrates spent his days in the streets of Athens. He talked to all people about what they believed in. He felt it was important to ask questions. He kept asking questions until people found their own answers. Athenian leaders did not like it when he questioned them. They thought Socrates was dangerous. At the age of 71, he was put on trial and sentenced to death.

Statue of Socrates outside the modern Academy of Athens

One of Socrates's most famous students was Plato. Plato opened a school called the Academy. He believed life should be guided by what is good, beautiful, and true. Plato was interested in politics. He believed that politicians should put the interests of the people before their own. He wrote about these ideas in *The Republic*. Plato wanted to split Athens

Artists in the 1500s imagined what the ancient Greek philosophy schools were like.

into three groups: warriors, producers, and philosophers. The warriors would defend the state. The producers would feed everyone. And the philosophers would make sure everything ran smoothly.

Plato is also known for writing about an island called Atlantis. According to Plato, the people on Atlantis grew greedy. Zeus decided to punish the people. In a single day and night, the island disappeared under the sea. Some people believe the story to be true. Or Plato may have invented the myth to use Atlantis as an example.

387 BCE
Year Plato began his school.

- The Greeks liked talking about knowledge.
- Socrates encouraged people to question everything.
- Plato was one of Socrates's students and continued Socrates's philosophical work after his death.

THINK ABOUT IT

Socrates encouraged young people in Athens to question laws. Leaders in Athens were unhappy with Socrates. They put him on trial for his actions. Why do you think leaders saw Socrates as a threat?

21

Ancient Greeks Advanced Science

Aristotle was a Greek scientist who was interested in the natural world. In the 300s BCE, he wrote about plants and animals. He filled books with his ideas and observations. He also studied weather patterns, forces, and motion. His ideas were studied for centuries after his death. Though many of his teachings were later shown to be wrong, he inspired many future scientists.

Because Greeks were interested in learning, many areas of science grew. Aristarchus was a student of Aristotle. He studied and wrote about the stars. He worked out the distances from the earth to the sun and the moon. He is best known for his ideas about how the planets move. He believed that the sun was the center of the universe. He said that the earth moved around the sun. Euclid was also a

great mathematician. He shared his ideas on geometry in *The Elements*. Students used his books for more than 2,000 years.

The Greeks used their scientific ideas to make practical machines. Archimedes was a student of Euclid's school. He once made a pulley to lift a

Aristotle was sent to study at Plato's Academy.

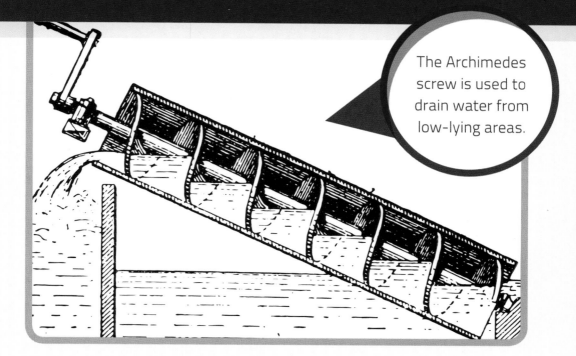

The Archimedes screw is used to drain water from low-lying areas.

ship singlehandedly. He also built a screw that worked like a pump. Water moved up the screw when it was turned. Some of Archimedes's ideas were used to make weapons. One of these weapons threw stones. Another could punch holes in the sides of ships.

13

Number of math texts Euclid wrote.

- Ancient Greeks were interested in science.
- Aristotle studied the natural world.
- Archimedes turned his ideas into machines.

ANCIENT GREEK VENDING MACHINE

Heron was a great Greek inventor. He used steam to make toys with moving parts. One of his toys was a bird. A jet of steam made the bird seem to fly. He also built what may be the first vending machine in history. At the top of his machine was a slot. A visitor to a temple placed a coin in this slot. Water then poured into a small cup below.

Wars Weakened Greece for Roman Conquest

From 431 BCE, the rival city-states Athens and Sparta began a series of conflicts. They fought on land and at sea for 27 years. The people of Athens hid behind their city walls. But a deadly disease swept through the city. It killed nearly one-third of the people. Although Sparta won, both city-states were much weaker than before.

In 359 BCE, Philip II became king of Macedonia in northern Greece. After conquering nearby regions, he set his sights on Athens and other Greek city-states. He wanted control of the Athenian ships to invade the Persian Empire. In 338 BCE, Philip became the ruler of Greece. When he died, his son Alexander took his place.

As a child, Alexander read about Greek heroes and was a student of Aristotle. He believed he was related to two heroes of Greek myth, Achilles and Heracles.

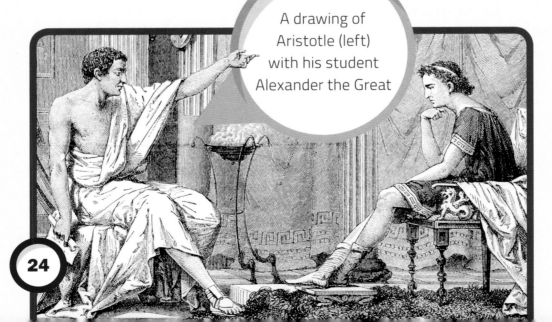

A drawing of Aristotle (left) with his student Alexander the Great

As ruler, he became known as Alexander the Great. He united the city-states of Greece. He then set out to finish what his father started. Alexander led the Greeks against the Persians. Greek ideas, language, and culture spread under his rule. Alexander and his army marched into Egypt and India. But some of his men grew tired of the fighting. They wanted to return to Greece. In 323 BCE, Alexander suddenly died. His vast lands were soon split up.

By 146 BCE, all of Greece came under the control of the ancient Romans. But Greek culture did not die. Its art, architecture, and religion became part of Roman culture. Great writing and theater continued through Roman poets, such as Virgil. He was inspired by Greek storytellers. Virgil's most famous poem, *The Aeneid,* was inspired by Homer. There were also advances made in medicine. People kept making beautiful art and buildings.

The Romans used art to merge Greek myths, such as stories about Heracles, with their own.

13
Number of years Alexander the Great ruled.

- The wars between Athens and Sparta weakened Greece.
- Greek culture spread under Alexander the Great.
- The Romans took control of Greece by 146 BCE.

The Greeks Changed the World

There are many ways the Greeks influenced the world. Many modern-day ideas about philosophy have their roots in ancient Greece. The works of Socrates, Plato, and Aristotle encouraged generations of people to question and investigate the world around them.

The government of the ancient Greeks is long gone, but traces of it remain. The idea that people should be judged by juries comes from ancient Greece. Although juries in US court cases have 12 people, the juries of ancient Greece were usually much bigger. Ancient Greeks also get credit for inventing democracy.

In 1896 CE, the Olympic Games were revived. They were held in Athens, Greece, that year, but now cities from all over the world can host the Games. One popular event is the marathon, a race of 26.2 miles. The marathon was not an event at the original Olympic Games, but it can still be traced back to the ancient Greeks. In 490 BCE, the Greeks defeated the Persians in a major battle. A runner traveled all the way from the site of the battle

Juries in the United States listen to evidence presented from the prosecution and defense before making a decision.

in Marathon to Athens to deliver the good news. Today's marathons celebrate that long-distance journey.

The Greeks also introduced new styles of architecture. Their temples were surrounded by large columns made of marble. Many of Washington, DC's buildings are influenced by Greek architecture. The Lincoln Memorial looks like a Greek temple.

Greek ideas about health also are important today. Hippocrates was a

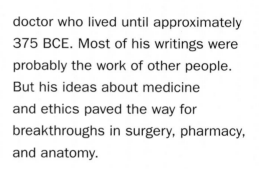

The Lincoln Memorial has columns on the outside of the building, just like ancient Greek temples.

doctor who lived until approximately 375 BCE. Most of his writings were probably the work of other people. But his ideas about medicine and ethics paved the way for breakthroughs in surgery, pharmacy, and anatomy.

PYTHAGOREAN THEOREM

Pythagoras was a Greek philosopher who lived until approximately 497 BCE. None of his own writings survive, but he greatly influenced later Greek philosophers, such as Plato. Pythagoras wanted to understand the world through mathematics. His theorem about right triangles is still taught in geometry classes today.

150,000
Estimated number of English words from Greek.

- The ancient Greeks influenced modern-day philosophy and government.
- The Olympic Games were revived in 1896.
- The Greek doctor Hippocrates paved the way for medical breakthroughs.

27

12 Key Dates

7000 BCE
People begin to permanently settle in Greece.

800 BCE
Greek city-states begin to appear; the Archaic Period begins.

776 BCE
The first Olympic Games are held at Olympia in the Peloponnese.

750 BCE
Approximate date the epic Greek poem *The Odyssey* is written.

507 BCE
Democracy begins in Athens, and only male citizens are given the right to vote.

500 BCE
The Classical Period begins.

480 BCE
Sparta and Athens unite to defeat the Persian invaders.

432 BCE
Construction of the Parthenon is completed.

431–404 BCE
Athens and Sparta fight a long war.

387 BCE
Plato founds the Academy in Athens.

338 BCE
King Philip II becomes ruler of Greece, and his son Alexander the Great takes over after Philip II dies.

146 BCE
The Roman Empire takes control of Greece.

Glossary

acropolis
A large hill in the center of a city with many important temples and buildings.

city-state
An ancient Greek city with its own government, laws, and armies.

colony
A place settled and controlled by people from another country.

culture
The language, beliefs, and traditions of a group of people.

democracy
A system of government in which the people have a say.

myth
A story people tell to explain their history.

ostracon
A broken piece of pottery used as a ballot.

peplos
A type of sleeveless dress worn by women.

philosopher
A person who is interested in the meaning of life.

polis
A Greek city-state.

For More Information

Books

Edwards, Roberta. *Where Is the Parthenon?* New York: Grosset & Dunlap, 2016.

Green, Jen. *Hail! Ancient Greeks.* New York: Crabtree Pub., 2011.

Kindley, Tom. *Heroes of the Night Sky: The Greek Myths behind the Constellations.* London: Cicada Books, 2016.

Nicolaides, Selene. *Gods, Heroes, and Monsters: Discover the Wonders of the Ancient Greek Myths.* New York: Barron's Educational Series, 2016.

Visit 12StoryLibrary.com

Scan the code or use your school's login at **12StoryLibrary.com** for recent updates about this topic and a full digital version of this book. Enjoy free access to:

- Digital ebook
- Breaking news updates
- Live content feeds
- Videos, interactive maps, and graphics
- Additional web resources

Note to educators: Visit 12StoryLibrary.com/register to sign up for free premium website access. Enjoy live content plus a full digital version of every 12-Story Library book you own for every student at your school.

Index

About the Author

Anita Yasuda is the author of more than 100 books for children. She enjoys writing biographies, books about science, social studies, and chapter books. Anita lives with her family in Huntington Beach, California, where you can find her on most days walking her dog along the shore.

READ MORE FROM 12-STORY LIBRARY

Every 12-Story Library book is available in many formats. For more information, visit 12StoryLibrary.com.